TRIVIA
OF THE CIVIL WAR

WILLIAM C. DAVIS

Designed by Philip Clucas
Featuring the Photography of Tria Giovan

MALLARD PRESS
An imprint of BDD Promotional Book Company, Inc.,
666 Fifth Avenue,
New York, N.Y. 10103.

CLB 2740
© 1993 Colour Library Books Ltd., Godalming, Surrey, England.
First published in the United States of America 1993 by The Mallard Press.
Printed and bound in Singapore by Kim Hup Lee.
ISBN 0 7924 5556 8

**MALLARD
PRESS**

INTRODUCTION

There was nothing remotely trivial about the Civil War – it was a bloody conflict that indiscriminately claimed the lives of young and old, rich and poor, educated and illiterate. It tore families apart, devastated whole towns and left in its wake wounds both physical and social that took years to heal.

The raw business tools of killing. Paper-wrapped "cartridges" spill from a cartridge box, while the copper percussion caps that fire the rifle lie beneath a soldier's leather cap box.

The record books and the eye of the camera, as well as telling something of the tragedy and carnage, have preserved for posterity images, facts and statistics that are trivial by comparison. Yet somehow it is these fascinating glimpses, these pieces of background information, that add a human dimension to what was an inhuman event. Trivial in the scheme of things, the letters from home, the personal possessions, the lesser known and often surprising facts, combine to give us a fuller appreciation of those harrowing times.

CHAPTER ONE

THE SOLDIERS

At a very minimum 2,778,304 men enlisted in the Union armies during the course of the war. Many enlisted more than once, while records of other enlistments is lost, so the overall figure can never be known with accuracy. Certainly more than two million individual men served the cause at one time or another.

There are no complete or accurate figures for Confederate enlistments.

Commonly accepted figures range from 600,000 to almost a million, but about 750,000 is probably closest to the mark.

Those enlisting came from widely varying backgrounds, especially in the Union. Free blacks accounted for 178,975 enlistments, Indians for another 3,530. Moreover, tens of thousands came from various ethnic groups recently immigrated to the North. English, Scottish, Welsh, and Irish made up the largest immigrant groups, followed by Germans, Hungarians, Poles, and Italians. In the Confederacy, native-born white males made up the over-whelming bulk of enlistments, though a fair number of Irishmen also joined the colors. Native Americans and Mexican-

LEFT: Colonel Hugh Garland of the 1st Missouri Infantry, shows very much the typical garb of a Rebel field officer.
FACING PAGE: The typical dress of the private soldier of the South is revealed in this photo of prisoners taken just after capture at Gettysburg.

RIGHT: A Civil War cavalryman might carry a considerable array of equipment, including his boots, a boot hook, blanket, spare shoes, his kepi or hat, gauntlets, a pistol or two like these French "pin-fire" pieces, a hoof knife (lying on the gauntlets), a leather cartridge case for his pistol (bottom center), a pair of hoof trimmers lying on the case, and a horse-shoeing hammer at bottom right.

BOTTOM: Quite literally millions of photographs were made during the war, most of them soldier portraits like these "ambrotypes," or tintypes of two Union soldiers. Generally they were framed in gutta-percha folding "union" cases with ornamental brass mats. No soldier wanted to go through the war without capturing his image in uniform.

Americans also contributed a few thousand to the armies west of the Mississippi, and in the last weeks of the war, after the raising of Negro regiments was authorized, a few hundred Confederate blacks also enlisted.

Despite the fact that both sides instituted conscription – the draft – the armies of blue and gray were overwhelmingly composed of volunteers. In the Union several draft acts resulted in 249,259 men being called up. However, a man could pay a monetary "commutation" to escape such service. Moreover, he could also pay another man to go in his place. From these and other causes, only one-fifth of the men conscripted – just 46,347 – actually donned a uniform, laying to rest Southern

accusations that the North was raising armies of conscripts.

In fact, the Confederates fielded far more men from their draft than did the Union. Theirs was America's first military draft, enacted April 16, 1862, and all told some 81,993 were conscripted.

They were mostly young men, the average age in the Union army being not quite 26. At least 127 Yankee soldiers were a mere 13; 2,366 were over 50. Confederate figures are too incomplete for a judgement, but the average was probably slightly higher due to more older men eventually joining the hard-pressed Southern forces.

The average Union soldier was just over 5 feet 8 inches tall, weighed a little more than 143 pounds, had brown hair, and blue eyes, and had been a farmer before the war. Confederates would have been almost exactly the same, excepting for a somewhat higher proportion of farmers. The

LEFT: A Yankee sergeant poses with his guitar. Any such instrument guaranteed that the owner would be a popular fellow if he could play. BELOW LEFT: Recruiting posters like this helped induce the millions who served to enlist, sometimes by appealing less to patriotic instincts than to desires to avoid the stigma of being drafted. BELOW RIGHT: A knapsack from the 5th New Hampshire displays some of an infantryman's usual kit, including cartridge box, bayonet and scabbard, canteen and kepi.

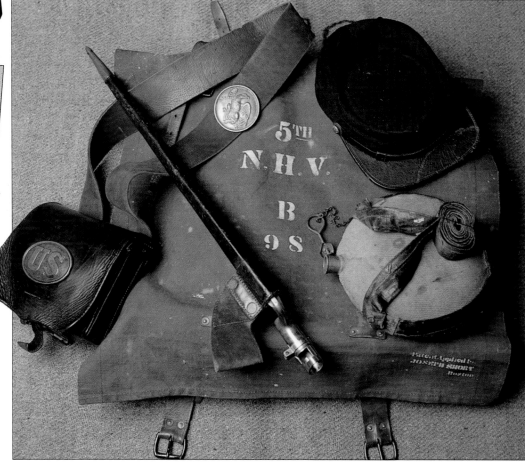

relatively light weight indicates how lean and fit men of the time were.

The tallest Yankee soldier was probably Captain David Van Buskirk of the 27th Indiana, standing over 6 feet 10 inches. The shortest on record was a 24-year-old Ohioan who stood just 3 feet 4 inches.

The tallest soldier of the entire war was a Confederate, Private Henry Thurston of Texas, who stood 7 feet, 2 inches, and was prone to accentuate his height even more by wearing a stovepipe hat.

This mass of men were organized into 3,559 different units in the Union Army:

Infantry regiments 2,144
Cavalry regiments 272
Heavy artillery 61
Engineers 13
Light infantry battalions 9
Artillery Batteries 432

FACING PAGE AND LEFT: A group of officers of the 3rd Missouri Infantry, U.S.A., pose at Corinth, Mississippi, in October 1863. They are typical-looking men, from the colonel seated at center to the lieutenants at far left and right. The man standing fourth from the left offers a bit of a mystery with his distinctly puzzling headgear. Also the sabers on display present quite a variety, revealing the officers' preference for arming themelves rather than accept standard government issue.

In the Confederate forces, at least 1,526 different units were organized. They included unusual outfits called "legions" that included infantry, cavalry and artillery, all within a single command, as well as a number of independent battalions and companies. Confederate units included at least the following:

Infantry regiments 642

ABOVE: Hundreds of thousands of slaves ran away to the Union armies, some to become soldiers and others to work as laborers or teamsters, like these men in Virginia.

THIS AND FACING PAGE: Part of the camp of the 153rd New York Infantry in winter quarters. One company stands drawn up for the camera. INSET BOTTOM LEFT: Confederate soldiers' kit from the Washington Artillery of New Orleans. INSET BOTTOM RIGHT: The hardee hat, standard Union issue. FACING PAGE INSET BOTTOM LEFT: An oilskin or rubberized case protects paper from the damp. Millions of letters were written during the war. FACING PAGE INSET BOTTOM RIGHT: Soldiers carried these images of loved ones off to war with them.

The statistics of the war revealed every sort of trial and hardship. The soldier at right stands proudly with the tattered flag of the 8th Pennsylvania, revealing the storm he and it have passed. BELOW LEFT: Some men were not so brave or patriotic, like this one executed in Virginia for rape. BELOW RIGHT: Thousands who faced battle had later to face being hospitalized, like these Yanks in Washington's Harewood Hospital. Most of them are there thanks to diseases like measles rather than due to the hazards of the battlefield. FACING PAGE: The ultimate cost faced by all soldiers has been paid by this Confederate of Lee's army in May 1864. More than a quarter million died in this way, fallen in battle.

Cavalry regiments 137
Artillery regiments 16
Artillery batteries 227

Loyalties were indeed divided. Every Confederate state except South Carolina sent organized white regiments into the Union armies. States like Missouri, Kentucky, Maryland, and even the District of Columbia, had units in both armies.

Attrition could be terrible in these regiments. Ideally, an infantry regiment began the war 1,000-strong. Of roughly that number, the 5th New Hampshire lost 295 to battle deaths. In a single engagement, the 1st Maine Heavy Artillery had 210 killed. The largest regimental loss in a single battle for any unit in the war was in the 1st Minnesota, which lost 224 killed and wounded at Gettysburg, out of 262 engaged: 85.5 percent!

The largest recorded unit loss in the Confederate forces was the 26th North Carolina, which had 708 killed, wounded, and captured, at Gettysburg, out of 880 engaged. The greatest loss in percentage of strength was probably the 1st Texas Infantry, which went into the fight at Antietam with 226 present, and lost 186 killed and wounded, more than 82.25 percent.

LEFT: Burial details had the woeful and often grisly task of collecting the bodies of the slain, like this boy, and hastily interring them in often makeshift graves.

During the course of the war the North suffered 360,222 deaths. Of those losses, 67,088 were killed outright in battle, another 43,012 died of wounds, and 224,580 died of disease. But men died of other causes as well; causes unforeseen when they enlisted. Almost 5,000 drowned. Murderers killed 520, and another 391 took their own lives. Federals executed at least 64 for varying crimes, and simple sunstroke killed 313. At least 275,000 Yankees were wounded.

Confederate battle casualties are imprecise, but best estimated at 94,000 killed in action or mortally wounded, and 164,000 died of disease, making a total of 258,000. The numbers of wounded reached at least 194,000.

Thus, a Union soldier stood a one in three chance of becoming some kind of casualty, a one in five chance of being killed or wounded, and the same chance of losing his life from any of a number of causes. For Confederates, almost two out of three could expect to become casualties, while more than one in four would be killed or wounded in battle, and there were odds of more than one in three of dying from any of a number of causes.

At least 200,000 Yankees deserted during the war, some more than once. In the South, 104,000 desertions are known.

At least 194,000 Union soldiers were captured and sent to prisons in the South, where 30,218 of them died of disease, malnutrition, and other factors largely beyond the control of their captors. Prior to the surrenders of the Southern armies, about 214,000 Confederates were captured in various actions during the war, and 25,976 of them died in captivity.

It was not a pleasant war.

ABOVE: The face of the Civil War was the face of youth, like this young Confederate officer.
FACING PAGE: Personal effects of an officer in a black regiment include his pocket diary for 1864, an Ames saber, his pocket watch and chain, a silver medallion, and his carte de visite photo of himself in uniform, all against the backdrop of his commission and papers.

CHAPTER TWO

THE GENERALS

ABOVE: The youngest general in U.S. Army history was Galusha Pennypacker, commissioned before he was 21. He is a major in this pre-1865 photo never before published.

In all, at least 1,008 men, North and South, were officially commissioned as generals during the course of the war. In the Confederacy there were 425 of them; in the Union 583.

The Union lost 47 generals killed in action; the Confederacy lost 77. Moreover, the South lost an additional 15 to other causes, two killed in duels, and one to suicide. The North lost 18 dead due to accident or disease, one murdered, and one suicide.

Of the Union generals, 217 were West Point graduates; 188, almost one-third, had no military training or experience at all. In the Confederacy, 146 were Military Academy graduates; 153, just over one-third, had no military education or experience.

Overall, the average age among the 425 Confederate generals was just 36 years, nine months. The oldest was 62-year-old Samuel Cooper; the youngest was William P. Roberts, just over 23 when given his stars.

The youngest Union general was Galusha Pennypacker, who, incredibly, was made a brigadier at age 20, before he was old enough to vote! The oldest was John E. Wool, born in 1784, and retired in 1863 at age 79. Overall, the average age among the 583 Union commanders was 37 years and six months.

The Confederacy recognized four grades of

general officer. There were 328 brigadiers; 72 major generals; 17 lieutenant generals; and eight full grade generals. In the North, only two grades were authorized through most of the war, with 132 major generals and 450 brigadiers. In 1864 U.S. Grant was made the North's only active lieutenant general.

The senior ranking general in the whole Confederate Army was not, as many think, Robert E. Lee. In fact, he began the war as the third ranking officer. Albert Sidney Johnston's commission as a full general predated Lee's, making him next senior. But forgotten old Samuel Cooper was senior to them all, though he never saw active service, spending the entire war on staff duty in Richmond.

Ironically, Cooper, like several other high ranking Confederates, was a native of the North. He was born in New Jersey. Johnston and John B. Hood, both full generals, were natives of Kentucky, which never seceded. John C. Pemberton, lieutenant general commanding the defense of Vicksburg, was

a Pennsylvanian, as was Josiah Gorgas, head of the Ordnance Department. Franklin Gardner, commander of the Port Hudson defense, was a New Yorker. In all nearly ten percent of Confederate generals hailed from the North.

Southerners who remained loyal to the Stars and Stripes sometimes achieved high rank for the

ABOVE LEFT: Confederate general George B. Crittenden gave ample proof that this was truly a "brothers' war."
ABOVE RIGHT: His own brother was Union Major General Thomas C. Crittenden, who served in the field against his sibling.

Union, most notably Virginian George H. Thomas, commander of the Army of the Cumberland and victor at the Battle of Nashville. But the overhwelming majority of Yankee commanders came from north of Maryland and east of Ohio.

At least one general fought on both sides. Frank Armstrong stayed with his U.S. Army commission long enough to fight in blue at First Manassas on July 21, 1861. Then he resigned and joined the Confederacy, eventually becoming a brigadier commanding cavalry. Justice McKinstry, a Union brigadier who would be cashiered for dishonesty, tried at first to get a Confederate commission, and only joined the Union when the Confederacy refused him.

LEFT AND FACING PAGE: Some of the personal military effects of one of the greatest Confederate generals, Robert E. Lee. His hat, binoculars, sword belt, and a presentation 1851 colt Navy .36 revolver. Ever loyal to his state, Lee had the Virginia seal on the buckle plate of his belt.

INSET: The general himself, Robert Edward Lee, in a photo taken a few years after the war, and showing the toll it had taken on him.

Cases of generals who had brother, fathers, or sons serving on the opposing side were too numerous to mention in detail. George Crittenden was a Confederate brigadier, his brother Thomas a Yankee major general. James McIntosh, C.S.A., killed at Elkhorn Tavern in 1862, was the brother of

ABOVE: The interior of Lee's field tent, showing his boots and saddle, and his mess chest with cooking apparatus.

BELOW: The war had father-son aspects, as with General Jerome B. Robertson, whose son Felix was also a Confederate general.
RIGHT: Robert Ransom of North Carolina entered the Rebel service as did his brother Matthew Ransom (far right), and both were destined to become Confederate generals.

Union General John B. McIntosh. James Terrill became a Rebel brigadier, while his brother William wore stars for the Union. Both would be killed in battle, James just one day before his commission took effect. Cavalryman "Jeb" Stuart's father-in-law, Philip Cooke, was a general in the Yankee cavalry, and he had a son, John, who became another Confederate general.

Many sets of brothers became generals on the same sides. Ben McCulloch and Henry E. McCulloch served the Confederacy from Texas; Robert E. Lee's sons Custis and William H.F. Lee both wore stars in their father's command. Howell and Thomas Cobb were both inexperienced politicians from Georgia whom Jefferson Davis made generals. Peter and William Starke came from Virginia, the latter being killed at Antietam. The Ransom bothers, Robert and Matt, both achieved distinction with the Army of Northern Virginia. Jerome B. Robertson and Felix Robertson were father and son generals from Texas. In the Union, Napoleon and John Buford of Kentucky served ably, as did David and William Birney, also from Kentucky. Then there were the

FACING PAGE BOTTOM RIGHT: General Philip St. George Cooke was the father-in-law of Confederate general J.E.B. Stuart. Both commanded opposing cavalry.

ABOVE: James McIntosh followed his sympathies into the Confederate army, and in 1862 he gave his life for the cause in the battle of Pea Ridge, or Elkhorn Tavern, in Arkansas.
LEFT: His brother was John B. McIntosh, who followed his conscience into the Union service, eventually rising to the rank of major general by brevet.

RIGHT: A fanciful artist's representation of the fighting at Port Hudson, LA, where the Rebel commander, General Franklin Gardner, was a native of New York.
BELOW: An obscure Colonel Thomas, one of thousands of colonels who hoped for promotion to the coveted rank of brigadier.
BOTTOM RIGHT: Confederate general Frank Armstrong actually served for a time in the Yankee army, at first.

FACING PAGE LEFT: The regulation frock coat of a Confederate general, this one belonging to Franklin Gardner. The bluish-gray fabric with buff standing collar, shows three gold stars surrounded by a wreath, the insignia the same for all grades of general.
FACING PAGE FAR RIGHT: a woodcut of General George A. Custer in 1863-4, showing the long, flowing blond curls for which he would be famous.

McCooks of Ohio: Alexander, Daniel and Robert all became generals, the latter two killed in the war, while cousin Edward also wore stars for the blue.

They were daring men. Nathan Bedford Forrest had 29 horses killed under him in battle, while he personally killed more enemy soldiers than any general on either side. They also had their share of cowards. Gideon Pillow would be tarred with that brush twice in the war, once for abandoning his command to be captured at Fort Donelson, and again at Stones River, when his brigade went into battle while he hid behind a tree.

They were also occasionally headstrong. Union Brigadier General Jefferson C. Davis – no relation to the Confederate President – shot and killed fellow General William Nelson in Louisville following an argument. In Arkansas in 1863, Confederate Generals John S. Marmaduke and Lucius M. Walker fought a duel that left Walker dead.

They were also tender, forgiving, and brotherly, even to enemies. When Simon Buckner surrendered his Rebel command to U.S. Grant at Fort Donelson,

Grant remembered a kindness done him years before by Buckner, and put his purse at the captive's disposal. When General Stephen D. Ramseur lay mortally wounded after the battle of Winchester, Virginia, in 1864, he was brought to a house and tended by his old West Point friends, now Union generals, including George A. Custer. Rebel General Joseph E. Johnston, who surrendered his army to William T. Sherman in April 1865, later acted as pall

bearer at the funerals of U.S. Grant and other Yankee generals, including Sherman himself, who had become a friend. Legend says that, standing bare-headed at Sherman's side in the rainy procession, Johnston caught the cold that led shortly afterwards to his own death.

Robert E. Lee, who spent his remaining years after the war as president of what is now Washington and Lee University in Lexington, Virginia, once threatened to dismiss from his faculty any professor who spoke ill of the man who had defeated him, General U.S. Grant.

CHAPTER THREE

THE WEAPONS

ABOVE: This Yankee cavalryman displays the weapons of his trade. He holds one Colt pistol in his hand, another in his belt, and a cavalry saber.

The most incredible array of edged weapons appeared on the fields of the Civil War, including, but not limited to: swords, knives, bayonets, lances, axes, machetes, dirks, daggers, rapiers, cutlasses, spears and arrows

Indeed, far more than this was carried in the marching armies, chiefly by Confederates, who had to make do with whatever weapons they could find or bring from home. Some even carried outmoded single-shot pistols with hinged knives mounted alongside the barrel, ready to be turned outwards to make a discharged gun into a thrusting weapon.

Surely the most unusual weapon of all never made it to the army. President Jefferson Davis was presented with a plan by an inventor for a steam locomotive with a number of scythe-like rotating knives spinning from the front and sides. Its inventor promised that it would kill thousands, so long as the Yankees were obliging enough to stand alongside the railroad tracks.

Reportedly the largest sword of the entire war was carried by Major Heros von Borke, the Prussian officer who rode through the war with "Jeb" Stuart's Southern cavalry. It was fully four feet long, and was more than twice the weight of a normal dragoon saber.

Despite all the attention given in training and in the popular imagination to the glistening bayonet

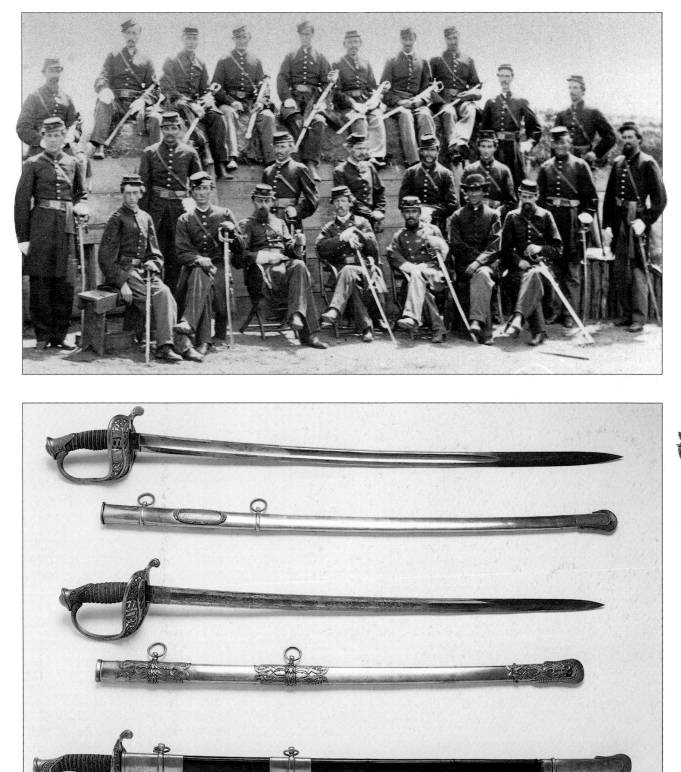

LEFT: A group of Union officers pose inside an earthwork fortification, each leaning on his saber. The colonel, lieutenant-colonel, and major are seated front row center.

BELOW: The massive sword carried by Major Heros von Borke rests at left. He rode with J.E.B. Stuart. Colonel William Carter's sits at right in contrast.

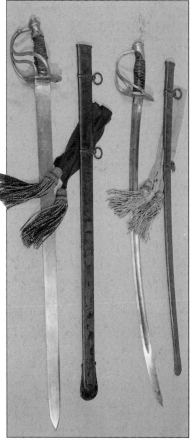

LEFT: A selection of sabers includes an 1850 field and staff sword at top, an 1850 presentation model in the middle, and a model 1850 foot officer's sword at bottom.

RIGHT: Just a few of the bewildering variety of handguns made and used North and South. At left is a Bacon Pocket revolver. An Evans derringer sits to right of it, with a Sharps four-barrel "pepperbox" just beneath. A true pepperbox lies at the top. Right of the Sharps is a Colt 1849 Pocket revolver, and to its right is an 1865 Remington New Model Army revolver. At far right is a Model 1851 Colt .36 Navy revolver.

BELOW: Some of the long arms carried by the men in Blue and Gray. At top is a Colt Model 1853 revolving rifle, used by sharpshooters. Beneath it is the Sharps carbine, and below that is a Burnside carbine, invented by General Ambrose Burnside.

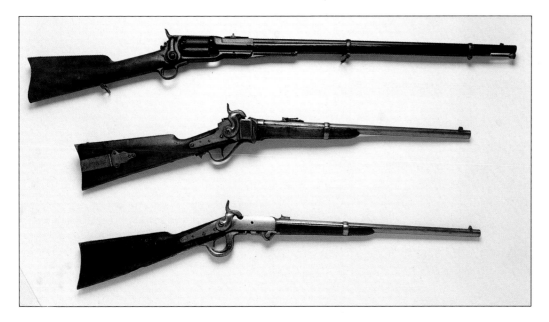

and the flashing saber, only about one soldier in 100 ever actually used an edged weapon in action.

The variety of rifles used was even greater. Caliber alone presented a bewildering array. Rifles as small as .32 caliber were used, and a few even smaller in some cases, while a few Confederates carried massive "chimneys" with a bore size of .75. The standards in the armies were .58 and .577 for the Springfield and Enfield rifles, chiefly used respectively by Union and Confederate forces.

The revolving rifle was used in a few Yankee outfits, chiefly sharpshooter regiments. It was nothing more than an enlarged Colt revolver, but proved dangerous to the man firing it thanks to the possibility of all six chambers going off at once.

One Union general, Ambrose Burnside, was more effective as an inventor than a commander.

Before the war he patented a repeating carbine that saw service with a number of Union cavalry regiments.

One of the most condemned inventions of the war was an exploding bullet, designed to go off after entering a man's body. It saw only experimental use, and was never widely adopted.

Hand grenades came into their own in this war, though most were nothing more than exploding cannon balls with special fuzes. The Ketcham grenade was a five pound oblong shell with a wooden tail and paper fins to help guide it straight when thrown. A plunger at the nose detonated the grenade when it hit the ground. The Confederates and Federals both manufactured varieties in which a strap or cord attached to the fuze was wrapped about the thrower's wrist. When he threw the grenade the cord went taut and pulled a pin, igniting the fuze as the grenade was passing through the air.

ABOVE: More of Billy Yank's weaponry, laid out on a regimental Stars and Stripes. A Colt .44 1860 New Model Army pistol sits top right, with a derringer and pepperbox beneath, a powder flask, bullet mold, caps, cartridges, and a Ketchum grenade at bottom left.

RIGHT: Pistols were not standard issue for infantrymen like this corporal in a black regiment. Some soldiers brought their own, or picked them up on the battlefield. Also, some photographers kept them as "studio" props, and the Colt Model 1849 in this soldier's hand is probably one such.

FACING PAGE FAR RIGHT: An idealized engraving of a Yankee infantryman leaning on an equally idealized – and therefore unidentifiable – rifle. Such a blending of romance with weapons of death was a unique feature of the Civil War.

FACING PAGE, CENTER BOTTOM: The savage revolver in this rakishly attired cavalryman's hand was a very effective, but relatively scarce, item in Union arsenals. It had two triggers – one to turn the cylinder and cock the gun, and another to fire it. The saber is regulation, but the dirk in his belt is definitely a personal affectation. His tent and effects can be seen in the left background.

LEFT: A close-up of the loading mechanism of the fearsome 144-round Volley gun. BELOW FAR LEFT: Regulation stacking for Federal muskets kept them clean and ready for action.

Pistols rivaled shoulder arms in their variety. Many men carried percussion single-shot models with detachable shoulder stocks that allowed for greater steadiness in aiming. In time, similar stocks were issued for many of the Colt .44 Army revolvers.

The largest pistol to see usage, and that limited, was the Colt .44 Dragoon or "Walker," the largest military handgun ever issued in America. It weighed nearly five pounds. Most were a holdover from the Mexican War.

ABOVE: Seacoast cannon in a former Confederate fort on the Virginia Peninsula in 1962. These smoothbores, small bore columbiads, were designed to repel enemy vessels.

FACING PAGE: Two 12-pounder gun-howitzers, known generally as "Napoleons," on the battlefield at Antietam.

Many soldiers carried tiny single-shot pistols and Derringers, though they were not standard government issue. A few also packed the antiquated "pepper-box" repeaters that had up to nine or more barrels in a large cylinder, the entire affair revolving with each shot.

The most unusual pistol was surely the LeMat revolver, which had up to nine chambers in a revolving cylinder, and carried beneath the barrel an 18-gauge shotgun tube. Confederate generals like P.G.T. Beauregard and Jeb Stuart favored the LeMat.

For raw firepower, nothing could match the "machine gun" inventions of the time. The Vandenburgh Volley Gun had up to 144 or more parallel chambers arranged like a honeycomb inside the cannon's casing. A single percussion cap would discharge all of the chambers at once. Its only wartime service was with Confederates in North Carolina.

The Requa Battery used the same principle, except that it had twenty or more rifle barrels arranged in a single horizontal plane. Special brackets held bullets for each, so that all could be

ABOVE: A rubble of artillery projectiles at Richmond's Tredegar Iron Works in the days after the city's fall in April 1865. Mortar shells are stacked in the background; canister and grape at front.

loaded at once. It saw some limited service with Union forces in South Carolina.

One Confederate cannon was manufactured with two gun tubes welded side-by-side, the idea being to fire two balls simultaneously, each connected by a chain to the other. Presumably they would cut a wide swath though Yankee ranks. In fact, the balls simply bashed into each other, or started spinning until the chain broke.

The largest cannon of the war was a massive 20-inch Rodman smoothbore, seacoast columbiad. It could hurl a shell weighing several hundred pounds up to ten miles or more. It never fired in anger.

The Gatling Gun, the most efficient and practical of the machine gun designs, only came into its own in the closing months of the war, and no more than a dozen or so saw action – mercifully.

ABOVE LEFT: Parrot rifle tubes being unloaded from Union barges in 1864-65 in Virginia. They were the most effective long-range big-bore rifled cannon of the war. ABOVE: The Union established experimental and manufacturing laboratories, like this one in Philadelphia, all across the North. LEFT: A host of experimental cannon designs emerged during the war, including this "wizard" gun firing the 900-IB projectile at front right.

CHAPTER FOUR

THE BATTLES

ABOVE: Robert E. Lee's last battle was one of words, negotiating his surrender at Appomattox. Thomas Nast, though not present, left this poignant sketch of the scene.

No one can ever entirely agree upon the exact number of engage-ments of the Civil War, in part because the definition of a "battle" is not in itself a fixed thing. They could range from the massive Fredericksburg, the greatest battle – in terms of numbers present – in the history of the hemisphere, to minute affairs involving no more than a dozen or so on either side.

The gleaning of War Department records collected after the war indicated that there were at least 10,455 operations that merit the name. They break down as follows:

Campaigns 2   Battles 76
Engagements 310   Combats 46

Actions 1026
Assaults 29
Skirmishes 6337
Operations 299
Sieges 26
Raids 64
Expeditions 727
Scouts 434
Reconnaissances 2532
Affairs 639
Occupations 82
Captures 79

Not only were the vast majority of actions of a small character, as reflected in the above, but also the majority took place not in Virginia, as most would expect, but scattered throughout the western states. The following shows where the fighting took

LEFT: A dramatic painting of the parapet of Fort Sumter in 1863 after hours of Yankee bombardment. The Confederate flag still flies in Conrad Wise Chapman's portrait, though the rubble caused by the pounding is quite evident. Sumter was reduced by war's end to little more than a hulk of broken masonry, though its Rebel defenders never gave up until Charleston itself was about to fall.

BELOW: The scene of two Rebel victories, Fredericksburg, Virginia, reveals in this 1864 image some Yankee tents in the distance. The fighting took place nearby, overlooking the Rappahannock River.

place in numbers of events:

Virginia 2154	Tennessee 1462
Missouri 1162	Mississippi 772
Arkansas 771	West Virginia 632
Louisiana 566	Georgia 549
Kentucky 453	Alabama 336
North Carolina 313	South Carolina 239
Maryland 203	Florida 168
Texas 90	Indian Territory 89
California 88	New Mexico Territory 75

Other states, like Indiana, Illinois, Ohio, Pennsylvania, and even Vermont, also had events, not least the massive Battle of Gettysburg, yet the total number in these states is too small to merit listing, amounting to fewer than a dozen each.

On December 13, 1862, the greatest number of men ever arrayed on a battlefield in this hemisphere met at Fredericksburg, Virginia, on the Rappahannock. Somewhere between 190,000 and 200,00 were present. The result was a bloody defeat for the numerically superior Federals.

RIGHT AND FACING PAGE: An engraving showing the typical fairy-tale notion of the appearance of battle, in this case the fighting at Chickamauga in September 1863. It was never this neat.

The bloodiest single day of the war came on September 17, 1862, near Sharpsburg, Maryland, along Antietam Creek. As many as 4,800 men died, and total casualties for both sides came to more than 26,000. More Americans lost their lives that day than in the D-Day landings at Normandy.

ABOVE: In sieges like these at Vicksburg and Petersburg, men turned gopher to protect themselves from enemy shelling, digging bomb-proofs like this one to serve as magazines, shelters, and sometimes even as quarters.

The bloodiest battle of the Civil War was fought at Gettysburg, Pennsylvania, July 1-3, 1863. At least 5,700 were killed outright, and total casualties came to 43,500 or more, almost a third of the 150,000 men engaged.

It would be hard to determine the most lop-sided victory of the war, but a major contender would have to be the battle of Sabine Pass, Texas, on September 8, 1863. A Confederate garrison of only 43 men, led by a 19-year-old lieutenant, drove off a

LEFT: MEN WENT INTO battle with a host of personal items not issued to them by their respective governments. This Yankee clothing went into the first battle of Bull Run on an enlisted man of the 1st Rhode Island Infantry. Only the kepi is regulation, and even it is the wrong color by later standards.

Yankee fleet of four warships and some 10,000 or more troops attempting to land, and disabled and captured two of the ships in the process.

Numbers are always difficult to ascertain with precision for Civil War engagements, but it appears that, in terms of numbers of men actually engaged, the most even battle of the war was the fight at New Market, Virginia, May 15, 1864. Federal General Franz Sigel had 3,745 infantry actively participating in the conflict. His opponent, Confederate General John C. Breckinridge, had 3,746! Breckinridge won.

The war's first major battle, First Manassas or Bull Run, saw the home of Wilmer McLean used as headquarters for several Confederate generals, and his property overrun by Rebel soldiers. Disgusted, McLean soon afterwards moved his family in an attempt to get away from the war. He moved to Apomattox Courthouse, only to have the armies find him once again, on April 9, 1865, when Robert E. Lee surrendered to U.S. Grant in McLean's parlor.

Some cities became battlefields almost daily. At least three major battles took place at Winchester, Virginia, and during the war the town changed hands at least 76 times.

The most decisive defeat ever inflicted on a Union army came at Chickamauga, Georgia, on September 20, 1863, when Confederates broke through the Yankee center and sent the bluecoats reeling from the field, only one corps holding its ground. Two months later the same armies met again, at Missionary Ridge, near Chattanooga, Tennessee. On November 25, the Confederate left

FACING PAGE: The so-called "Stone House" on the Warrenton Turnpike witnessed much of the 1st Bull Run fighting at a distance. During and after the battle it was used as a hospital for wounded of both sides. Its wooden floors still show bloodstains to this day.

RIGHT: In the aftermath of Gettysburg, the United States Sanitary Commission set up quarters like this camp to lend assistance in burying the dead and tending to the living. It distributed medicines and reading materials, brought civilian nurses to the men, and often provided spiritual comfort as well.

BELOW: An utterly fanciful artist's idea of the climax of the Battle of Gettysburg, including a Union countercharge that never happened. But this was the face of battle as seen by the families and politicians back home.

crumbled and the most humiliating Rebel rout of the war ensued, again with only one corps holding its ground.

Incredible coincidence stalked many of the major battles. At First Manassas, Stones River, Chickamauga, and several others, both opposing commanders had almost identical battleplans before the fight.

Definitions of victory were often in the mind of the beholder. At Antietam, universally acclaimed as Lee's first defeat, the gray chieftain had in fact gotten himself into so tight a trap that the mere fact of standing his ground against his ineffectual opponent George B. McClellan, then getting his army away to safety intact, represented a far greater "victory" for Lee than for McClellan's putting an end to the invasion of Maryland. At Chancellorsville, the next May, hailed as Lee's greatest triumph, the win

came at the expense of the accidental death of Thomas J. "Stonewall" Jackson. Many would claim that the loss of Jackson lost the war.

At Fort Sumter, the first hostile engagement of the war, Lieutenant R.K. Meade helped operate one of the guns in the fort, returning fire against the attacking Southerners. A few weeks later he resigned and enlisted in the Confederate Army, dying for his new cause in 1862.

Generally acknowledged as the last land fight of the war, the skirmish at Palmito Ranch, Texas, on May 13, 1865, was a Confederate victory. Ironically, all but one of the Confederate armies had by this time surrendered.

ABOVE: A woodcut depicting fighting between Confederates and a Negro regiment in Louisiana, perhaps at Port Hudson. Such actions settled the debate as to whether blacks would fight.

LEFT AND FACING PAGE: A scene of the inevitable consequence of battle. This May 1863 photo shows Confederate dead behind the stone wall on Marye's Heights at Fredericksburg.

INSET LEFT: One of the most deadly, yet glorious, moments in battle, in this case the climax of "Pickett's Charge" at Gettysburg.

INSET BELOW: For years after a battle the dead kept coming out of the ground for reburial.

CHAPTER FIVE

SPIES AND ESPIONAGE

ABOVE: Loretta Velasquez made incredible post-war claims of daring spy service. No evidence exists to show that she did anything at all, making her a colossal humbug.

Most of what is "known" about Civil War era spies cannot be "known" with certainty at all. They left few reliable accounts. Most of them, trying to remain hidden in the shadows, covered their tracks too well to follow, and others, for whom lies and exaggeration became a defense, could not stop exaggerating when they later recounted their adventures.

The Confederacy inaugurated America's first governmental "Secret Service." Major William Norris was originally in the Rebel signal service, but soon ran his own tiny, and official, clandestine operation.

When the war began, almost everyone in Washington was "spying" for one side or the other. Senators, congressmen, postal officials, even Supreme Court officials, were passing information south to the Confederates. Most of it was useless.

The war's first spy to achieve notoriety was Rose Greenhow, who slipped information to Confederates along Bull Run, advising that a Yankee army was about to march against them. It was pointless, because everyone in northern Virginia could have told them the same thing.

At first, women seemed especially attracted to the romantic notion of spying. Besides Greenhow, Bettie Duvall slipped information to the Rebels,

LEFT: Pauline Cushman did do brief and quite ineffectual spy work that succeeded only in getting her caught and nearly hanged. In later years she made a shabby living on the theater and sideshow circuit by dressing in uniform and delivering melodramatic lectures with exaggerated accounts of her largely fictional adventures.

ABOVE: A minor Confederate spymaster, Jacob Thompson was stationed in Canada to incite insurrection in the North and hatch plots for releasing prisoners from Yankee camps. None ever succeeded.

ABOVE: One of the most effective partisans of all time, Colonel John S. Mosby, the "gray ghost" of the Confederacy, defied and baffled the Yankees for years. ABOVE RIGHT: A group of Mosby's raiders, men of the 43rd Virginia Partisan Rangers.
RIGHT: The most notorious Yankee opponent of the Union war effort was Clement L. Vallandigham, the so-called copperhead.

wrapped inside the curls of her hair. Pauline Cushman made bumbling attempts at gathering intelligence for Union forces in Tennessee, was caught, and made a career of recounting her adventures after the war. Loretta Velasquez – if that was her real name – completely invented a wartime career as a spy, wrote a book, and lectured about it for years. Her only war service was possibly a few months in Richmond as a prostitute.

Union intelligence was left to outsiders early in the war. General McClellan hired the Allen Pinkerton Detective Agency to gather intelligence on Lee's army in Virginia, and Pinkerton produced consistently exaggerated and unreliable estimates of the enemy's numbers and movements. One of the war's best spies, Timothy Webster, was a Pinkerton man, who reportedly produced great information until caught and hanged.

In the West, as in the East, individual Federal generals hired their own spies. Ormsby Mitchell in Chattanooga arranged for James Andrews to conduct his fabled railroad raid into Georgia in 1862, culminating in the Great Locomotive Chase. Andrews, too, was caught and hanged.

Not until the Union War Department authorized Colonel George Sharpe to engage in espionage activities, did the North have a "professional" spy corps. He ran the Bureau of Military Information for the Army of the Potomac from 1863 until the end of the war.

Espionage accounted for much of the clandestine activity of spies, and the most successful single achievement was probably the mysterious explosion at City Point, Virginia, Grant's supply base in the 1864 Petersburg operations. A Rebel secret service captain had planted a bomb amid Union ammunition stores.

Perhaps the most effective spy network of the war belonged to Norris, who established the so-called "Doctors' line" from Richmond, through Maryland, to Washington. Manned by secessionist physicians, it depended upon their need – as doctors

Readers thrilled to the romanticized dime-novel adventures of heroines-turned-spies, especially when illustrated like the scene of an arrest at left, or the even more dramatic midnight ride of some petticoat patriot braving all to deliver some vital information, lower left.

ABOVE: The reality was less lurid, and more deadly. John Yates Beall was hanged after the war for leading an attempted piracy on Lake Erie in 1864.

RIGHT: Another of the self-aggrandizing heroines was Virginian Belle Boyd, who did some good service, but not as much as she claimed after the war.

FAR RIGHT: A genuine spy of merit was Elizabeth Van Lew of Richmond, who wheedled information out of Rebel authorities and smuggled it to the Yankees.

BELOW: Some spies ended their days as did John Wilkes Booth, murderer of Lincoln. He, too, was an amateur Confederate agent of sorts.

FACING PAGE: Scouts and guides with the Army of the Potomac in 1862. Such men were often distrusted even by their own side.

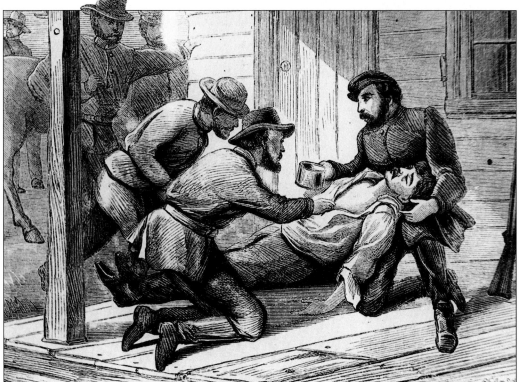

– to be out on the roads at all hours. They carried information, mail and medicines, from the North to the South.

One Rebel spy, Thomas Conrad, spent almost the entire war in Union lines, in Washington, gleaning information about troop numbers and movements.

Probably the Union's most notorious clandestine operator was Lafayette C. Baker, a self-aggrandizing adventurer who was never very effective, but ruthlessly went after suspects, and filled Washington's prisons with them. He it was who finally tracked down John Wilkes Booth after the murder of President Lincoln.

Little is known of the degree of secret service penetration deep behind the lines. In one instance, in Richmond, Samuel Ruth, operator of the Richmond, Fredericksburg & Potomac Railroad, fed information to Colonel Sharpe and intentionally held up Confederate rail movements on his line.

Confederates brazenly established a large delegation of spy and espionage agents in Canada,

centered at Toronto and Montreal, from which bases they sent operatives into the North. There were attempts to burn New York City, free prisoners in Northern prison compounds, even – some accused – to spread smallpox in the North and destabilize Yankee currency by disrupting the gold supply.

Disloyalty ran rife North and South. In the Union, organizations like the Knights of the Golden Circle attempted to encourage desertion and resistance to the draft, as well as assisting escaped Rebel prisoners. Their great hope was to see parts of Illinois, Indiana, Ohio and other northwestern states break away from the Union and either join the Confederacy, or form a nation of their own.

Disloyalty was ever present in the Confederacy. The Order of the Heroes of America flourished in

BELOW: Another group of Army of the Potomac scouts and guides. They often doubled as impromptu spies, and were just as likely to be dealt with as such by the foe, even when not spying. Like most spies, their names are today forgotten.

Virginia and North Carolina, downing telegraph lines, burning bridges, and feeding information to invading Union commanders.

Spies, when caught, were generally doomed to death. Best known of all was Sam Davis, a Tennessee boy caught with information in his possession. He refused to save his life by revealing what he knew, and went to the scaffold. Women spies, though caught more often than men, invariably escaped death thanks to the 19th-century inhibition about executing women.

RIGHT AND FACING PAGE: The ultimate Confederate espionage agents paid the ultimate price for their role in the plot to kidnap Lincoln that turned to assassination. No execution was more ignominious than hanging, a fate reserved for spies especially.

No attempt has ever been made to ascertain the number of clandestine operators, North and South. From the nature of their work, most remain unknown. Nevertheless, the number on either side during the course of the war probably exceeds 1,000, including scouts, mail couriers – called blockade runners – and conventional spies. No tally exists of how many lost their lives, but a fair estimate would be 40-50 on each side.

When the war ended, so did military information gathering, not to be revived for decades.

CHAPTER SIX

THE NAVIES

ABOVE: Two jaunty tars on the USS *Hunchback*, a Yankee river gunboat. They stand beside a 12-pounder Dahlgren rifle.

Only about one Yankee in twenty went into the Navy; total enlistments amounting to just 132,554, of whom about 5,000 joined the Marines.

In the Confederacy, by contrast, a mere one in 200 entered the waterborne service. Total enlistments are unknown, but in 1864 the entire Confederate Navy counted but 3,674, including the few hundred in the tiny Marine Corps.

Unlike the armed land forces, the navies of both sides had a heavier concentration of men with some nautical background before the war, and drew more heavily from the Atlantic and Gulf seaboard states. Indeed, the navies of both sides were entirely composed of pre-war prof-essionals and wartime volunteers. Men were not conscripted into the navies.

No exact total of naval "engagements" has ever been compiled, but it would be tiny by comparison with the experience of the land forces. No more than half-a-dozen "fleet" actions took place on the Mississippi, and as many more in the Confederate harbors. The overwhelming majority of naval actions involved Yankee ships against stationary Confederate forts or shore batteries. Confederate vessels were chiefly engaged in attacking unarmed merchantmen on the high seas.

Casualties were light by comparison with the

LEFT: A converted Staten Island ferry boat turned into a Union river gunboat, the *Commodore Barney* plied the coastal waters of Virginia and North Carolina during the war.

BELOW: Another New York ferry turned into a gunboat, the USS *Morse* served throughout the war, doing excellent service on the Atlantic rivers and sounds. Such vessels were the Union's initial answer to the problem of paucity of warships in 1861.

armies, too. Just over 1,800 Yankee sailors lost their lives as a result of battle, while another 3,000 died of disease, meaning that a Yankee seaman stood only a one in 28 chance of losing his life. Of those lost, drowning claimed 308, and scalding by burst steam boilers claimed another 342, showing the special hazards of the service. Wounds were inflicted upon an additional 226, meaning that, overall, a Union tar stood a one in 19 chance of becoming a casualty.

LEFT AND FACING PAGE: A selection of the tools of the Civil War sailor's trade includes the boxed chronometer on gimbles at lower left, a sextant to its right, a pair of calipers lying on the cloth, and the ever-present telescoping glass.
BELOW LEFT: The tailor-made dress blue uniform of a New York seaman. The embroidered star insignia on the sleeve shows his rank as seaman first class.

Confederate casualty figures are too sketchy to permit compiling a total. While the raw numbers would be less than in the Union Navy, the percentages lost would be considerably higher, thanks to many more Rebel ships being sent to the bottom in action.

Neither side began the war prepared for a naval contest. In January 1861 the Union had but 90 vessels, and 50 of those were unserviceable, being either incomplete in their shipyards, laid up for repairs, or obsolete sailing vessels. Lincoln had a

ABOVE: The tragedy of brother against brother struck in the navies, too. Captain Percival Drayton of the U.S. Navy was brother to Confederate General Thomas Drayton.

BELOW RIGHT: The first admiral, David Glasgow Farragut, the union's premier naval commander. He was a Tennessean by birth, yet remained loyal to the flag he had served since childhood.

BELOW RIGHT: A cross-section view of the interior of a *Passaic* class monitor. The armored pilot house sits atop the turret, the whole turning on a pivot on the keel. The turret interior was a bedlam in battle.

RIGHT: One of the war's most dramatic naval episodes was the repulse of a Yankee fleet and landing attempt at Sabine Pass, Texas, on September 8, 1863. Desperately outnumbered Confederates captured the USS *Sachem* at left and the *Clifton* at right and drove off the rest.

FACING PAGE TOP: A very fanciful woodcut of the CSS *Virginia's (Merrimack)* casemate during battle. The British Armstrong guns were not used on this ship, and the casemate was considerably less roomy.

FACING PAGE BOTTOM: The Confederacy's best-known naval commander was Captain Raphael Semmes, standing at center aboard his famous commerce raider CSS *Alabama*. Not a particularly effective shipboard leader, he was still a dreaded raider on Yankee commerce.

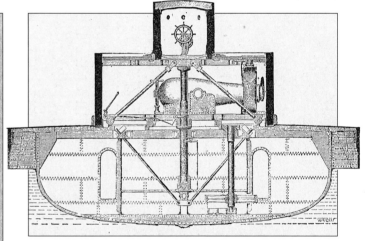

mere three modern steamships immediately at hand, most of the rest being absent on station at sea.

During the war the Union would construct 208 new warships and purchase another 418. Those purchased would include old Staten Island ferryboats, converted into river gunboats, and even private yachts.

The Confederate Navy began with nothing but what it could capture in navy yards in the seceding states. Through purchase and construction, the South eventually acquired perhaps as many as 500 vessels, though the overwhelming bulk of those were ineffectual light steamers and riverboats,

tugboats, and even small sailing vessels, few of them able to mount more than a bow gun.

By war's end, Lincoln's navy had at least 3,500 guns mounted on the decks of ships controlling virtually every navigable river in the country, and ringing the Southern coastline, as well as patrolling the oceans after commerce raiders.

At their best, Confederate ships probably never exceeded 600 mounted naval guns at any one time.

The average seaman in both navies had almost as great a likelihood of seeing action on land as at sea. So-called naval "brigades," frequently no more than a few gun crews, were often sent ashore to help in the attack or defense of land fortifications. Confederate naval and marine forces participated in several engagements on land during the Petersburg siege. At Port Hudson and elsewhere along the Mississippi, Yankee gun crews left their vessels to man cannon.

Infantrymen in the Confederacy could not infrequently find themselves called on to turn

"webfoot." In the defense of Vicksburg in the summer of 1862, Kentuckians of the Orphan Brigade left their places in the lines to work as gunners and coal heavers on the ironclad CSS *Arkansas*.

Controlling the blockade of Southern ports was the Union's chief concern on the water. In all, Federals estimated that they captured 1,504 blockade runners. In fact, the best figures indicate that only 136 were captured, and another 85 destroyed, out of almost 300 in the blockade trade. Total attempts to run the blockade and reach Confederate ports with goods from abroad numbered 1,300, with about 1,000 of them succeeding.

The largest fleet action of the war is the virtually unknown Battle of Plum Run Bend, Tennessee. On May 10, 1862 eight unarmored and ill-armed

LEFT: Summer dress – white uniform made of cotton, trimmed in blue, and with the straw hat allowed for summer wear.

BELOW: A deck officer with telescope on the watch for Rebel blockade runners.

FACING PAGE TOP: An artist's depiction of the Union river fleet running a gauntlet of fire from Confederate river batteries at Vicksburg on the Mississippi. It was one of the most daring and dramatic moments of the war on the rivers.

FACING PAGE BOTTOM: An inaccurate artist's representation of the Rebel commerce raider CSS *Florida* at Mobile, Alabama. It was second only to the *Alabama* in the number of prizes taken.

Confederate gunboats attacked a fleet of seven Federal gunboats. Two Yankee boats were rammed and sunk. Four Rebel vessels were neutralized, and the Southerners had to withdraw.

The trauma of brother-against-brother struck the navies as well as the armies. Captain Franklin Buchanan, commanding the Rebel ironclad *Virginia* in its attack on the Union fleet at Hampton Roads, Virginia, on March 8, was firing at his brother

LEFT AND FACING PAGE: The smallest of the Civil War armed services in both armies was the Marine Corps. Men like these U.S. Marines at Washington's Navy Yard in 1864 saw only limited service on shipboard or ashore.

LEFT: Old captain Franklin Buchanan, shown in U.S. uniform before the war, was the Confederacy's fightingest ironclad commander. He captained the CSS *Virginia* in her first battle in 1862, and later the *Tennessee* in her only battle in August 1864.
ABOVE: The so-called "ghost ship" of the Confederacy, the CSS *Shenandoah* sits in dry dock in Australia. Cut off from word of Rebel surrender, she kept taking prizes for months after the end of the war, not giving up herself until November 1865.

McKean Buchanan, an officer aboard the USS *Congress*, one of the ships sunk in the battle. In the Federal attack on Port Royal, South Carolina, on November 7, 1861, Commander Percival Drayton brought his gunboat in closer to Fort Walker than any other vessel, knowing full well that the fort's commander was his brother, General Thomas Drayton.

ABOVE: The Rebel raider *Alabama* met her end in battle with the USS *Kearsarge* off Cherbourg, France, on June 19, 1864. Heavily outgunned and slow due to poor engines and a fouled bottom, the *Alabama* (in the distance) was sunk in little over an hour.

ABOVE RIGHT: A painting depicts a blockade runner with Confederate colors flying, attempting to outrun a Yankee warship.

RIGHT: The ruins of the U.S. Navy Yard at Norfolk, Virginia, following its recapture by Union forces. It was here that Confederates converted the hulk of the *Merrimack* into the mighty ironclad *Virginia*.

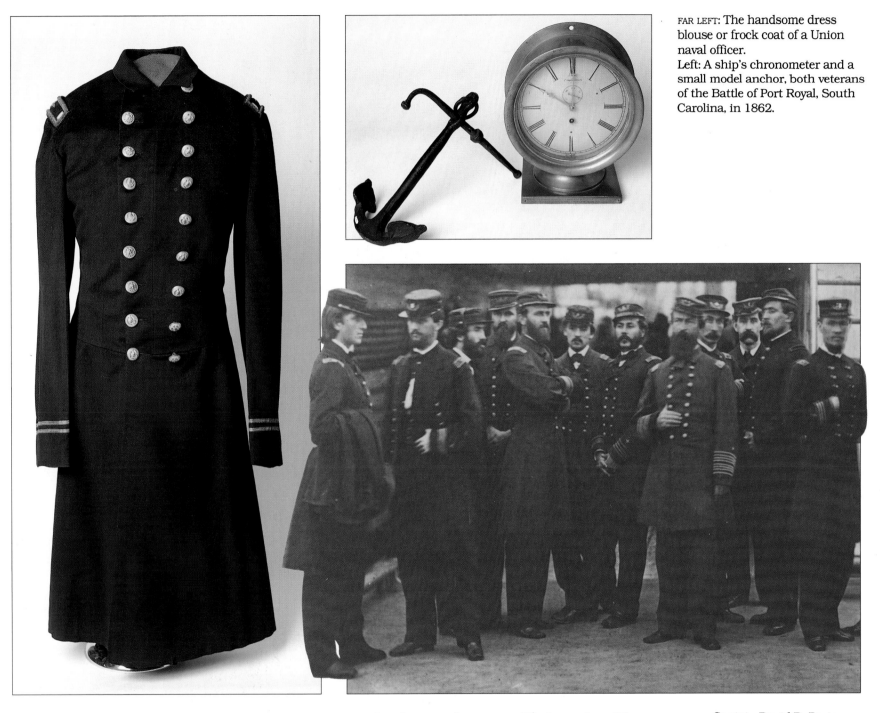

FAR LEFT: The handsome dress blouse or frock coat of a Union naval officer.

Left: A ship's chronometer and a small model anchor, both veterans of the Battle of Port Royal, South Carolina, in 1862.

Captain Sidney Smith Lee was one of the Confederate Navy's senior commanders. His brother was General Robert E. Lee. In the North, the Porters made the war a family affair, with David Dixon Porter becoming Grant's chief naval lieutenant, and his brother William "Dirty Bill" a prominent ironclad commander on the Mississippi. The Porters'

step-brother was the premier Yankee sailor of them all: Admiral David G. Farragut.

The last hostile shots fired came from the commerce raider CSS *Shenandoah* on June 28, 1865, when she captured eleven whaling vessels in the Bering Sea. She did not learn that the war was over for another five weeks.

ABOVE: Captain David D. Porter stands in the center, with long beard, surrounded by officers on his staff with the North Atlantic blockading squadron.

ABOVE: Samuel A. Cooley was one of a host of
enterprising photographers who took their cameras
into the field to record the drama of Americans at
war with themselves.